Oxford Learning Centre
#203 1595 McKenzie Avenue
Victoria BC V8N 1A4
Phone: 250-477-5550
oxfordlearning.com

TCR 5947

Finish the Picture

180+ Stickers Inside

ST P

Also Includes:
• Award
• Ribbon Sticker
• Reward Chart

Teacher Created Resources

Managing Editor
Ina Massler Levin, M.A.

Editor
Eric Migliaccio

Contributing Editors
Sarah Smith
Kristine Smith

Creative Director
Karen J. Goldfluss, M.S. Ed.

Cover Design
Tony Carrillo / Marilyn Goldberg

Teacher Created Resources, Inc.
6421 Industry Way
Westminster, CA 92683
www.teachercreated.com
ISBN: 978-1-4206-5947-4
©2007 *Teacher Created Resources, Inc.*
Reprinted, 2012 (PO5294)
Made in U.S.A.

Teacher Created Resources

This book belongs to

_____

Ready·Set·Learn

Get Ready to Learn!

Get ready, get set, and go! Boost your child's learning with this exciting series of books. Geared to help children practice and master many needed skills, the *Ready·Set·Learn* books are bursting with 64 pages of learning fun. Use these books for . . .

 enrichment   skills reinforcement   extra practice

With their smaller size, the *Ready·Set·Learn* books fit easily in children's hands, backpacks, and book bags. All your child needs to get started are pencils, crayons, and colored pencils.

A full sheet of colorful stickers is included. Use these stickers for . . .

- decorating pages

- rewarding outstanding effort

- keeping track of completed pages

Celebrate your child's progress by using these stickers on the reward chart located on the inside cover. The blue-ribbon sticker fits perfectly on the certificate on page 64.

With *Ready·Set·Learn* and a little encouragement, your child will be on the fast track to learning fun!

Dalmatian

Directions: Put spots all over the Dalmatian.

Rocket

Directions: Draw smoke and flames behind the rocket ship.

Flower

Directions: Add leaves to this flower.

6

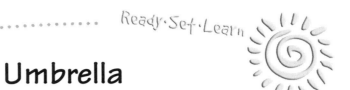

Umbrella

Directions: It's raining! Please hurry and finish drawing this umbrella!

Hot Air Balloon

Directions: Draw a giant hot air balloon.

Doughnut

Directions: This yummy doughnut needs a hole in the middle!

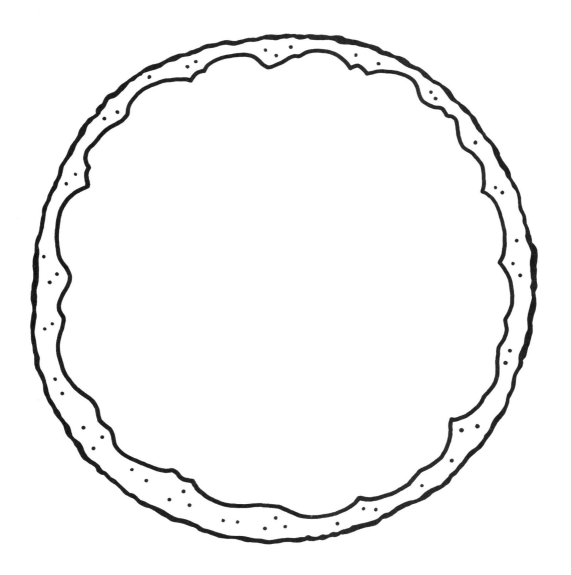

House

Directions: Build a house. Add a door and another window.
What else can you add?

Complete the Plane

Directions: This plane needs another wing. Add it on.

Finish the Flower

Directions: Draw in the missing petal.

Finish the Tree

Directions: Where's the tree trunk? Draw it in.

High Hat

Directions: Create a special hat for Ralph.

Mailbox

Directions: Draw the post this mailbox sits on.

Gift

Directions: Decorate this gift with a bow and colorful paper.

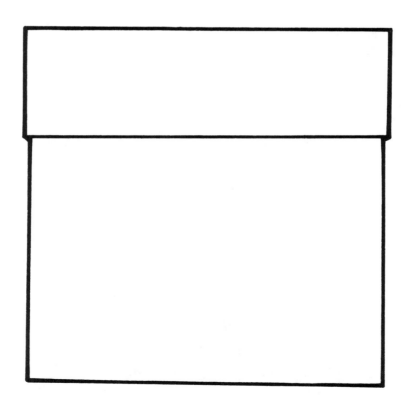

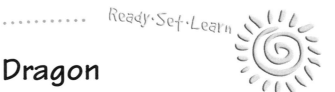

Dragon

Directions: This dragon needs wings to fly and fire coming from his mouth!

Tree

Directions: Put more leaves on the tree. Does it have fruit?

Diver

Directions: Give silly Sam a diving board.

#5947 Finish the Picture

Bird

Directions: Parrot? Toucan? Hummingbird? Give this bird a beak.

Docking

Directions: Help chain the ship to the dock.

Giraffe

Directions: This funny giraffe needs a neck.

22

Pear

Directions: Are you hungry? Finish drawing this pear.

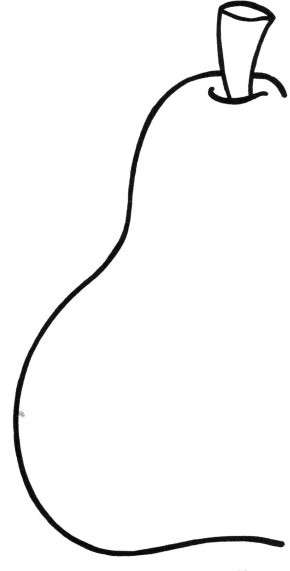

Running

Directions: Help Nancy run fast. She needs legs.

Ladder Rescue

Directions: Finish the ladder so Amy can put the baby bird back in its nest.

Spider

Directions: Give the playful spider eight long legs.

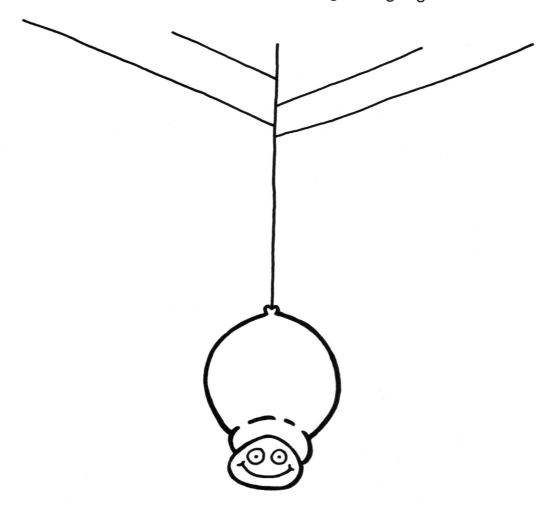

26

Pony

Directions: Give the pony something to jump over.

Bath Time

Directions: Draw a tub so this wet dog can finish his bath.

28

Butterfly

Directions: Give this little butterfly two big wings.

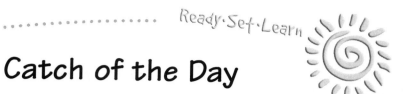

Catch of the Day

Directions: Draw what you think this fisherman will catch.

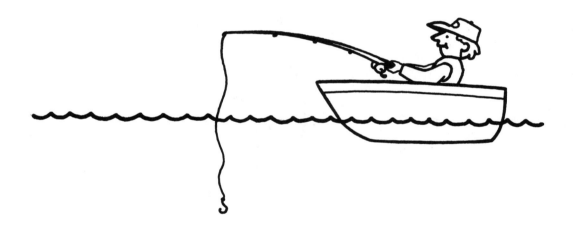

Finish the Bicycle

Directions: Find what's missing and draw it in.

Finish the Sign

Directions: Fill in the missing letter.

Nest

Directions: Fill this nest with colorful eggs.

Kitty

Directions: Little kitty is looking outside. What does she see?

34

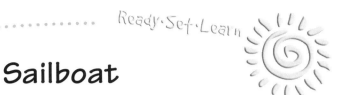

Sailboat

Directions: Decorate the sail and finish drawing the sailboat.

Teddy Bear

Directions: Finish the teddy bear. Give him a face.

Stamp

Directions: Finish this giant postage stamp.

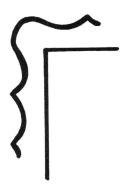

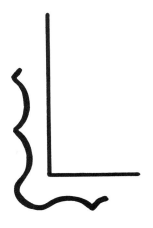

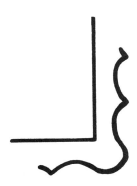

Jack-O'-Lantern

Directions: Turn this pumpkin into a jack-o'-lantern by adding a face.

Fish Fins

Directions: Give this playful fish some fins.

Heart

Directions: Finish the heart shape. Can you make it a valentine?

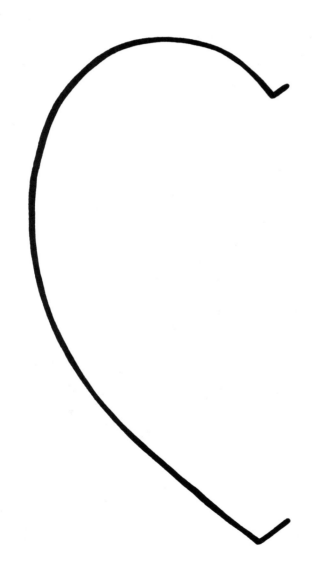

Night Time

Directions: Finish the moon. Can you add some stars?

Monster

Directions: This funny little monster needs a head.

Flower

Directions: What kind of flower is planted here? Draw your favorite bloom.

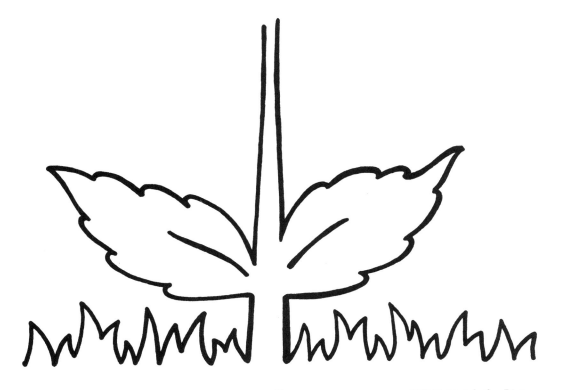

Porcupine

Directions: Cover this porcupine with sharp quills.

Queen

Directions: Give this queen a beautiful crown.

Snowman

Directions: Finish building this snowman. Add more snow.

Skier

Directions: Put a ski on each of Daniel's feet.

Sheep

Directions: Add more wool to this fluffy sheep.

48

Zebra

Directions: Put stripes on this wild zebra.

Monkey

Directions: Give this monkey a tail so she can swing from the tree.

50

Carrot

Directions: Finish drawing this healthy carrot.

Fish Bowl

Directions: Complete the fish bowl. Can you add more fish?

Shark

Directions: Give the smiling shark more sharp teeth.

Baseball Bat

Directions: Give David a good baseball bat.

54

Jump Rope

Directions: Draw Amanda's jump rope.

Finish the Man

Directions: Should he have hair? A moustache? A beard?

Stairs

Directions: Draw stairs so Alex can feed his cat.

Car

Directions: Give the car some wheels.

58

Book Cover

Directions: What is your book about? Design a cover.

Circus

Directions: Give this circus elephant a colorful drum to stand on.

Space Creature

Directions: Put a space creature inside the flying saucer.

Build a Building

Directions: Finish constructing this appartment building.

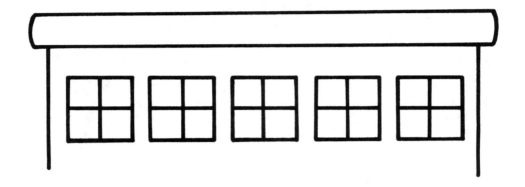

62

This Award
Is Presented To

_____

for

★ Doing Your Best

★ Trying Hard

★ Not Giving Up

★ Making a
   Great Effort